Walks in
Cordell Country

Chris Barber

Blorenge Books
1996

First Published 1996

ISBN 1 872730 11 6

© Chris Barber

Blorenge Cottage, Church Lane, Llanfoist
Abergavenny, Gwent, NP7 9NG. Tel: 01873 856114

Printed by Final Expert
Union Road Industrial Area,
Abergavenny NP7 7RQ
Tel: 01873 859899

" *The Garndyrys furnaces are silent now; mere skeletons of greatness that nature by constant effort, is striving to obliterate. And it is difficult to believe, as one stands on the crest of the Keepers' road that this was once a thriving community, a little town of people who lived their lives on the edge of a golden valley, who laughed and cried and brought forth children; who made iron of a quality incomparable; who sent her sons abroad to teach the art; whose sister town of Blaenafon sent her sons to Staffordshire to build new ovens, and as far abroad as Philadelphia...*"

Alexander Cordell 1959

Limestone Checker's Cottage, near the Blaenafon to Pwll-du tunnel

CONTENTS

ACKNOWLEDGEMENTS

I would like to thank everyone who has helped in the writing of this book which is based on my original publication entitled 'Cordell Country'. In particular I thank Alexander Cordell for providing the inspiration, writing a foreword and for giving me permission to include some quotations from 'Rape of the Fair Country'.

Also I am greatly indebted to Michael Blackmore who spent considerable time producing the illustrations and continues to share my enthusiasm for this subject. Mike and I enjoyed many fascinating hours discussing the detailed requirements for the artwork and his very special knowledge of the subject made him the ideal artist to undertake this work.

To Mike and Mollie Johnson I give my thanks for proof reading the completed manuscript.

PLEASE NOTE

All the routes described in this book are undertaken at the individual's own risk. The author / publisher cannot be held responsible for any accidents. Sensible footwear and waterproofs are advisable for the hill walking involved in following these routes. Walkers are also advised to use this guide book in conjunction with Ordnance Survey Map Sheet 161, 1:50,000 (Abergavenny and the Black Mountains). But the Sheet SO 21/31 (Abergavenny) 1:25,000 Pathfinder Series is particularly recommended.

SPELLING OF PLACE NAMES

Generally I have utilised the Ordnance Survey spelling shown on the 1:50,000 map sheet 161 in the route descriptions. But in his novel 'Rape of the Fair Country' Alexander Cordell spells Garnddyrys as Garndyrus, which occurs in some of the quotations.

FOREWORD

The following foreword was kindly written by Alexander Cordell for my original publication entitled 'Cordell Country' which was published by Blorenge Books in 1985.

In 1954 I unloaded on to an unsuspecting public my first novel, one which was supposed to set the Thames on fire. In fact it earned just one-and-sixpence less than the royalty advance of £75 paid to me by the unfortunate publisher.

My form of transport in those days was a pedal-assisted auto-cycle which took me daily from Llanellen village to my work as a Civil Servant. I set about trying to be a better Civil Servant, but failed because the writer's bug began to bite me again. And one winter's night saw me standing near the Old Victoria Inn wondering what bomb had hit this area. It was clear that something had violated this once fair country.

A man came walking with a bicycle out of the cold moonlight and he said his name was Parry; that he was a local postman on his way to visit his sister. I asked him what had happened to the place he called Garndyrus.

"Jawch, mun - terrible things have happened up here, don't you know?" I said I didn't, and Mr. Parry suggested that I should meet him the next evening at The Rolling Mill, a pub in Blaenafon. Next evening I was there at the appointed time, but Mr. Parry did not come. Some colliers, wondering at the stranger in their midst, engaged me in conversation: it isn't that the Welsh are nosey, they only want to know what's happening. I told them I was waiting for Mr. Parry, the postman.

"Duw", exclaimed a collier, "haven't you heard, mun? He died last night on his way to see his sister".

And so began scores of interviews with the old people whose tales of Blaenafon's past breathed life into *Rape of the Fair Country* . I wrote the book at white heat, scarcely altering a chapter: in between spells of writing I studied at the University of Wales, Aberystwyth and befriended every available librarian; more, I suddenly discovered that hand in hand with the tale of the mountain town went the last bloody revolution in Britain, the Chartist Rebellion, when men like John Frost a hundred years before their time, fought and suffered for the Six Point Charter - five of which we enjoy today in freedom.

Now thirty years later, my task as author of the book has long been ended, but Chris Barber, by introducing the solitary explorer or group to the paths and the lonely places where Iestyn Mortymer lived has done more than bring the story and its characters to life; he has succeeded in clothing an ancient skeleton with the flesh and blood of living history. Let the dry as dust historians bend us to their graphs and statistics, but it is given to creative people to hear the cry of a child trapped underground, or the sound of Welsh choirs echoing down the Sunday streets of a Welsh town. Myths and legends become living entities when a sixteen stone mountain fighter shivers when one mentions fairies. All the love and sacrifice that supported and upheld our forbears is reborn in the mind and heart of a solitary walker.

The Puddlers' Arms was a small inn situated on the Keeper's Road, just above Fiddler's Elbow. Ironworkers travelling down to Abergavenny and back must have sunk many a quart in here. Unfortunately the building was demolished many years ago and this drawing was based on a photograph of the ruined inn taken by Alexander Cordell in 1955.

Cordell Country is more than a travelogue; it stands in a higher dimension, recapturing, as it does, the spirit and industry of a people who worked with fire; who raised dirt monuments to generations unborn; who travelled with specialist knowledge from Garndyrus and Blaenafon, to build the coke ovens of Philadelphia and the furnaces of Andrew Carnegie in Pitsburgh.

Go down into the valley of old Garndyrus and hold in your cupped hands the cinders of their long dead fires and they will tell you of themselves...Read this tale, and you will hear the voices of these lost people calling on the wind...you can, I assure you.

Alexander Cordell

INTRODUCTION

Cordell Country was inspired by the historical novel 'Rape of the Fair Country' by Alexander Cordell. He based his story on the iron forge of Garnddyrys where a small village on the western slopes of the Blorenge was inhabited by a hard working community whose lives for a period of about fifty years were linked with this almost forgotten site.

The Mortymer family who are the main characters in the novel would have lived on the other side of the hill in Shepherd's Square near the Blaenafon Ironworks. From there it was just a short walk to the crest of the Turnpike road where one can look down into the valley of the Usk. A track led down from here to the Garnddyrys Forge and Rolling Mill where Hywel and Iestyn Mortymer worked twelve hours a day for six days a week. Iestyn started work there at the age of eight which was later than many of the children of that time. His father Hywel was a forge expert on the books of Crawshay Bailey the Nantyglo ironmaster and on loan to Garnddyrys.

Iestyn's sister, Morfydd scrubbed floors at the manager's house in Nantyglo in the mornings and worked afternoons and evenings down the Coity Pit.

"They thought a lot of Morfydd in Nanty... for she had quick fingers with bleeding when the children were caught in the trams, and she could deliver a baby underground as well as any doctor."

Since 1979 I have lived in the village of Llanfoist, beneath the brooding mass of the Blorenge and during the early years of the 1980s while I was undertaking regular walks across these bracken clad slopes I found myself imagining Cordell's characters walking these same paths. I pictured the hillside scarred by industry and imagined the sounds of horse-drawn trams, the roar of the furnaces and the whine of the rolling mill at Garnddyrys.

"The mountain was shuddering to the forge hammers of Garndyrus, and faintly on the wind came the plaintive singing of the Irish haulers. Llanfoist farms were sleeping in the pit-black darkness below, their blind windows winking at the stars, and Abergavenny was a town of dead, strangled by the ribbon of the Usk that gleamed and flashed in the scudding moonlight".

Such is the descriptive power of Alexander Cordell. Read 'Rape of the Fair Country' and 'This Proud and Savage Land' for yourself and you will be able to appreciate the historical and romantic associations of the locations that appear in his novels. Stand for example, by the Balance Pond near Pwll-du and imagine young Iestyn Mortymer having a scrap with Moesen Jenkins for *"...fighting by the Balance Pond was the custom and everything there being convenient for bruising: near home in case a man had to be carried, a gallows head with an oil lamp on it so you could see who you were hitting; and three feet of mud for the loser".*

Visit Llanfoist Wharf and conjour up a picture of the Garnddyrys annual outing when the village folk desended in trams down the steep inclines on the front of the Blorenge. Imagine a hundred laughing people piling into the waiting narrow boats for their annual June outing to Newport Fair.

"Down to Llanfoist Wharf we went, where a gang of broody Irish were waiting by a string of barges, and into them we went as excited as little children. The band came down next, with the beer and food after them, and Will Blaenafon and Rhys began to load it aboard while the children garlanded the barges and horses with summer flowers. Tomos Traherne climbed on to the prow of our barge and lectured us on how to behave in Newport; urging us to keep away from the gin-shops and beer-houses, which he said, were the scourge of a decent community.....Prayers, then, and thanks to the ironmaster who had given a sovereign or two to make all this possible, and Tomos blew on a horn. The horses were whipped up and away down the canal we went with our barge leading."

If you have the energy, ascend the steep incline above to reach Hill's Tramroad which snakes around the western slopes of the Blorenge and discover for yourself the site of the Garnddyrys Forge and the ruins of the village. Picture the women hanging out their washing or scrubbing their front steps whilst men stand smoking clay pipes in doorways and children play 'tag' in the street.

Make your way past Pen-fford-goch pond to reach the ruins of Blaenafon Ironworks and the workers' houses in Stack Square. Nearby was North Street, where the Company Shop was located next door to the infamous Drum and Monkey Inn.

"The masters always paid out in the beer-houses...for the beer-houses were owned by the masters too, and their paymasters always arrived late so that a man could drink on credit for hours before getting paid, and then be too drunk to count it."

Follow the mountain road to Brynmawr and head for Nantyglo where the mighty ironworks of the Bailey empire once stood. This was said to be the greatest iron-works in the world at one time and not far away is the site of Ty Mawr, once a grand mansion owned by Crawhay and Joseph Bailey. Nearby, gaze up at the round towers built by the Bailey brothers to shelter them and their families in times of trouble. The towers were fortified and kept stocked with food for the ironmasters were constantly concerned that their own workers might rise up against them.

Listen to the Redcoats marching in pairs from Brynmawr to Coalbrookvale and Nantyglo on a mission to keep the peace. On the hillsides above the valleys the Chartists are gathering for torchlight meetings to hear speeches from *"men like Henry Vincent who could sway a thousand men with a phrase and change the politics of women with a song."*

Think with sadness of the death of Hywel Mortymer - splashed by molten iron and half buried by bricks when a furnace split open and then wander across the lonely moors of Mynydd Llangynidr to a remote cave said to be used by the Chartists as a meeting place and an amunition store. Here they manufactured *"pikeheads and spears that were to wrest power from the aristocracy and give it to the people."*

Finally, picture the scene described in the closing chapters of Cordell's novel when thousands of men are marching down the Gwent valleys to overthrow the establishment and take possesion of Newport.

"Men from Garndyrus and Blaenafon, Coalbrookvale and Abertillery, Brynmawr and Nantyglo; wild men, starving men, soldiers with military bearing on the march to freedom."

Since the publication of 'Cordell Country' in 1985 many changes have taken place in the area. The 'Cordell Country Inn' has been opened, the name of which was inspired by the title of my book and for some years it displayed a sign painted by Michael Blackmore which reproduced the cover of the book 'Cordell Country'. Unfortunately one sign was stolen as a souvenir and another vandalised so these can no longer be seen.

Blaenafon Ironworks has been much restored and guided tours of the site are now available. Big Pit has also been established as a unique mining museum and a steam railway now runs from just beyond Big Pit to the Whistle Inn at Garn-yr-erw.

At Nantyglo the site of Ty Mawr, Crawshay Bailey's mansion has been excavated and the adjoining Round Towers restored. The towers were for a few years open to the public but sadly the owners no longer allow visitors access.

Clydach Ironworks has been excavated and a century of debris and undergrowth cleared away to reveal the substantial remains of a fascinating ironworks dating back to the latter years of the eighteenth century.

Blaenafon town holds an annual festival offering a range of events and attractions designed to bring visitors to the town and a considerable amount of money has been well spent on restoring the Workmen's Hall.

In 1989 Newport celebrated the Centenary of the Chartists' attempt to take the town by storm and the acceptance in later times of the principles and demands of their charter. A sculpture has been placed outside the Westgate Hotel to commemorate the events that took place on 4 November 1839.

On the north side of St Woolos Church a memorial stone has been erected to honour the fallen Chartists who lie there in unmarked graves and it is significant that in 1987 the Labour Party adopted the red rose as their symbol. This being due to the fact that red roses were left on this Chartist burial site for many years on the anniversary of their deaths. The custom has been revived and maintained by members of Newport Local History Society.

Many areas of dereliction have been transformed during the last two decades by an extensive landscaping and tree planting programme which has made the South Wales Valleys green again. The discovery of industrial remains and the study of social conditions in the hard times of 19th century Britain has caught the imagination of a large number of people and the area around Blaenafon is one of the most rewarding and fascinating areas to explore.

Visit Dorset and you will find 'Thomas Hardy Country'; Devon has 'Lorna Doone Country'; Howarth in Yorkshire is the heart of 'Bronte Country'; while on the border of Wales one can visit 'Kilvert Country'. There are also many more examples of locations that are visited by people from all over the world, who come seeking atmosphere and literary associations.

Compiling 'Cordell Country' was a most enjoyable project and my endeavours, undertaken more than ten years ago have been rewarded by the fact that the book was read and used by large numbers of people who returned time and time again to explore this fascinating area. Educational parties, in particular have found the book most useful and many schools have used it as the basis for environmental studies relating to the period of the Industrial Revolution.

Numerous letters of appreciation were also received from a wide assortment of people, from locals to visitors who have travelled here from distant parts. Some who came here to walk for pleasure and enjoy the beautiful scenery. Many came to study the industrial history of the area, whilst others who have read and re-read 'Rape of the Fair Country' seek out the romantic associations of Cordell's characters.

'Walks in Cordell Country' has been compiled to replace the original guidebook which was published in 1985 and has now been out of print for several years. It not only updates the previous material but it is also intended as a continuing tribute to the work of a much appreciated novelist who has given pleasure to so many people.

Recently, the new unitary authorities of Torfaen, Blaenau Gwent and Monmouthshire took up the 'Cordell Country' theme with the publication of a car trail linking sites mentioned in Alexander Cordell's novels that relate to the area surrounding Blaenafon and Brynmawr.

It had been my hope eleven years ago that the local authorities would give support to such an idea, with for example the erection of road signs bearing the words 'Welcome to Cordell Country'. Similar signs can certainly be found in other parts of Britain such as 'Catherine Cookson Country' in honour of famous local novelists.

Tourism is very often based on the historical and literary associations of an area and this is certainly a way to give a much needed boost to the economy of such places as Blaenafon, Brynmawr and Nantyglo.

Chris Barber,
Llanfoist, 1996

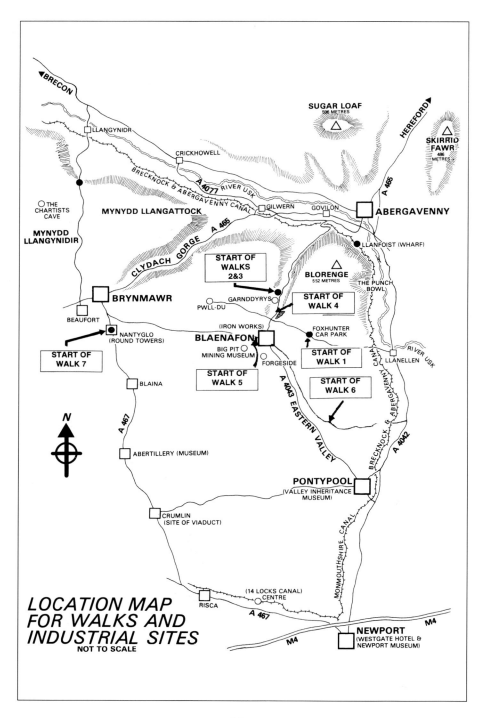

LOCATION MAP FOR WALKS AND INDUSTRIAL SITES
NOT TO SCALE

Hill's Tramroad at Pwll-du Quarry   Chris Barber 1990

The Blorenge and the five arches of Llanfoist Bridge.

" The Blorenge is rendered interesting on many accounts. It forms a termination to the great mineral basin of South Wales, and it is situated on what was formerly termed 'The Wilds of Monmouthshire'. Here terminates the valley, Afon Llwyd, named from the stream running through it. From its bowels, the Blaenafon, the Garnddyrys and in the same measure, the Nantyglo Iron Works, extract their wealth."

John White 1887.

WALK 1
From Blaenafon to Llanfoist
Allow (5 Hours)

This is a linear walk so it is recommended that you position an extra car at a suitable spot in Llanfoist village and then drive to the starting point in the other car(s). Otherwise catch a bus to Blaenafon and walk back.

Start from the Foxhunter Car Park which is situated about half-a-mile off the B4246 on the old Llanaellen road near the two tall radio masts (SO264108)

1. **Walk down the road towards Blaenafon for a few yards and then go left to follow a path to the right of the tall masts, heading towards some telegraph poles**.
   On the skyline to the left can be seen Carn Defaid (literal translation - Carn of the sheep). This is a Bronze Age burial mound where a large pile of stones probably covers an urn containing the ashes of some long forgotten local chieftain.

2. The track descends towards Blaenafon over an opencast landscape.

It was here that the ironstone deposits were once removed by 'scouring'. This involved extracting the minerals (which fortunately lay close to the surface) by first removing the turf and then clearing away the top soil by releasing water from above. A lake was formed by constructing a simple dam and when the dam was breached the water surged down and scoured the soil away to reveal the iron ore. About 3 tons of ironstone were required to make one ton of iron ore.

'This spot and its vicinity produce abundance of iron, with coal and limestone and every article for smelting the ore; the veins lie in the adjacent rocks, under strata of coal, and are from three and a half to seven or eight inches in thickness; they differ in richness, but yield, upon an average, not less than forty pounds of pig iron to one hundred weight of ore.'

Archdeacon Coxe 1801

Site of ironstone scouring above Blaenafon.   Chris Barber 1984

3. Join a stony track which meets the B4246 just above a cattle grid. Follow a grass verge on the left towards Blaenafon, passing the Rifleman's Arms on the left which may be of interest to you after the walk! Take the next road on the right and after about 50 yards go down a lane on the left.

4. At a bend by some garages, pause and look down on the remains of the Blaenafon Ironworks. Now follow the road around to the left. Turn right down some steps, go past the front of York House and then descend beside the fence surrounding the ironworks to reach a pavement. Follow it down to the entrance gate.

Blaenafon Ironworks 1799. Drawn by Sir Richard Colt Hoare.

Blaenafon Ironworks (SO 249093) was established in 1789 by Thomas Hill and Thomas Hopkins who leased the land from the Earl of Abergavenny at a rent of £1,300 per year for a 21 year term. It cost £40,000 to build and in 1790 the furnaces started producing pig iron which was initially transported to Newport by mule. Six years later the Monmouthshire Canal was opened between Newport and Pontnewynydd. This was linked with Blaenafon Ironworks by a six mile tram road down the Eastern Valley.

The ironworks had been operating for ten years when Sir Richard Colt Hoare made his well known engraving. The works expanded rapidly during the Napoleonic wars and by 1815 it was the third largest ironworks in South Wales. The biggest were Cyfartha and Dowlais at Merthyr Tydfil.

Archdeacon Coxe came here during his tour of Monmouthshire in 1799 and described the scene as follows:-

"At some distance the works have the appearance of a small town surrounded with heaps of ore, coal and limestone enlivened with all the bustle and activity of an opulent and increasing establishment.

The view of the buildings which are constructed in the excavations of the rocks is extremely picturesque, and heightened by the volumes of black smoke emitted by the furnaces. The coal is so abundant as not only to supply the fuel necessary for the works, but large quantities are sent to Abergavenny, Pontypool and Usk.

Although these works were only finished in 1789, three hundred and fifty men are employed, and the population of the district exceeds a thousand souls. The hollows of the rocks are strewn with numerous habitations, and the healthy ground convert-ed into fields of corn and pasture."

Thomas Hopkins died in 1789 and his son Samuel, on inheriting a large sum of money, decided to build a fine house for himself which he called Ty Mawr (Big House). Samuel was a popular man in Blaenafon and the town mourned his passing when he died in 1816. His sister Sarah constructed a school in his memory and reg-ularly taught in it.

In due course, Thomas Hill's son who was also named Thomas, arrived in Blaenafon to help his father run the ironworks. This young man made quite an impression on the town with his extravagant lifestyle but he was also very arrogant and soon became unpopular. However his life was shortened by drink and rich liv-ing and by 1827 both of the Thomas Hills were dead. Then along came the next in line who was yet another Thomas Hill and he took on Robert Wheeley the works manager as his partner. They ran the concern together until 1836 when it was taken over by Robert William Kennard.

By 1840 the works had expanded rapidly and when the travel writer Nicholson came here on his 'Tour of Wales' he described it as follows:-

"At the works of the Blaenafon Iron Company, five furnaces are all in blast, blown with cold air and six others erecting. This mineral property is one of the best and most valuable in the County of Monmouth, and these works have been distinguished for the superior strength and general excellence of their iron. These five firnaces produce about 400 tons of cast iron per week, and about one half of which is refined, and part of it made into cable iron, and the remainder is sold for tinplates and foundry work. This company is erecting extensive forges and rolling mills."

1843 was a disastrous year for the Blaenafon company, summed up by the follow-ing comment in the 'Monmouthshire Merlin':-

"The present state of the iron-trade annihilates hope, we see nothing but ruin before us and behind us. The trade must refine within its proper limits, but how that is to be effected - who are to stand, who are to fall - what is to become of the unem-ployed - how starvation is to be arrested, and the ruin of thousands averted - are questions beyond our province to unravel, but which must be met boldly in our face because they are not to be avoided - they are already at our door."

Mr. Ashwell, a civil engineer had been appointed to build three new furnaces and blast engines and the stone balance shaft at the end of the furnace yard. However he spent so much money that the capital of the company soon vanished and the works came to a stop. Ashwell then left for pastures new and the owners had to raise fresh capital. The works was then put under the management of Henry Scrivenor who during his term of employment wrote a useful book entitled 'History of the Iron Trade'.

Unfortunately the works still did not prosper and Mr. Scrivenor was replaced in about 1847 by Richard Johnson, a brother-in-law of William Crawshay. But once again the works came to a stop and fresh capital had to be raised. The management was then placed in the hands of a committee consisting of Thomas Hill, Robert Wheeley and Philip Jones, a banker who represented the Herberts of Llanarth.

The Balance Tower at Blaenafon Ironworks.   Chris Barber 1993.

Blaenafon Ironworks in 1895.   Picture supplied by Francis Keen.

The 60 ft high stack rising above the workers houses that were named after it was demolished in 1912.
Picture supplied by Francis Keen.

The 'Big Arch', Blaenafon Ironworks.   Chris Barber 1989

REMAINS OF THE IRONWORKS

The remains of the Blaenafon Ironworks were nearly swept away in a proposed land reclamation scheme during the early 1960s, but at that time there was talk of a film being made of 'Rape of the Fair Country' and it was decided to keep the site intact so that it could be used as a set. Unfortunately the film was never made but thankfully these important remains have been preserved as a heritage site and it is regarded as the finest example of and 18th century ironworks in Europe.

Michael Blackmore's drawing shows the remains of two of the blast furnaces. There were five furnaces in total and they were built into the hillside so that they could be easily charged from above. In the early days the furnaces were worked with open tops; the waste gases being allowed to escape into the air and at night the whole neighbourhood was illuminated. In later years the gases were collected and utilised for heating the hot air stoves and steam boilers.

The furnaces were originally fed by hand but at a later date they were mechanically fed by an ingenious system of tip-trams moving on rails along the top edge of the furnaces.

Blaenafon Ironworks 1983.

The Balance Tower

This tower which dominates the site, operated in a similar manner to the balance shaft at Pwll-du Quarry (described later in this book). Pipes carried water into a container which by virtue of its weight lifted a tram loaded with pig iron straight from the casting house to a higher level where it was then transported by rail to Garnddyrys Forge for further attention. The water in the container at the bottom of the tower was then drained away and the weight of the descending tram returned the container back to the top of the tower.

Stack Square at Blaenafon Ironworks.   Chris Barber 1996.

Stack Square

The two facing rows of four roomed cottages were built in about 1789 to accomodate the skilled workers who had been hired from the Midlands. At a later date the central connecting terrace was constructed and the Company offices were located on the ground floor. On the upper floor, dormitory accomodation was provided for the single workers.

According to the 1851 Census, 84 people lived in the square and they were no doubt all employed by the Blaenafon Ironworks Company. As many as ten people lived in one of these small cottages and one couple actually raised no less than nineteen children here.

The group of houses takes its name from a 60 ft high stack which once stood on the plinth which can be seen in the centre of the square and was connected to a steam engine which supplied the blast for the furnaces. The stack was demolished in 1912.

Shepherd Square

Nearby used to stand another row of cottages known as Shepherd Square and this was where Alexander Cordell placed the home of the Mortymer family in his novel 'Rape of the Fair Country'. It was situated at the south end of Staffordshire Row and' was similar in layout to Stack Square with the houses built on three sides of a court.

Shepherd Square and North Street in about 1960.

Other Dwellings

The workers all lived in company houses which were built in terraces and some-times back to back which saved space and time and enabled the builders to make the best use of the sloping ground. River Row was occupied by the colliers. Iron workers resided near their furnace at Stack Square, Shepherd Square, North Street and Staffordshire Row. In particular many of these houses were occupied by specialist workers who had been 'imported' from the Midlands to work at Blaenafon.

The men who worked with horses lived in Stable Yard, Stable Row and Upper Stable Houses. Engine drivers and the mechanics of the new steam age were to be found in Engine Row and Mechanics' Row. These men were very proud of their trades and such identity was very important to them. It even controlled the position in which they sat in chapel.

Bunkers' Row used to stand opposite the Rifleman's Arms and consisted of two terraces built end to end in the late 18th century. They were demolished in October 1982. These cottages stood near the Blaenafon Brickyard which supplied refractory bricks for furnace linings. At one time the employees were mainly women who had to work in very grim conditions.

Blaenafon Brickyard workers in 1880s.   Picture supplied by Francis Keen.

Bridge Houses

When Archdeacon Coxe visited Blaenafon in 1789, his companion Sir Richard Colt Hoare made a drawing which shows a bridge where the five supporting arches had been converted into workers' dwellings. Coxe described the scene as follows:-

"The want of habitations for the increasing number of families, had occasioned an ingenious contrivance: a bridge being drawn across a steep dingle for the support of a railroad leading into a mine, the arches which are ten in number, have been walled up and formed into dwellings."

Tramroad bridge with arches filled in to provide 'houses' for industrial workers.

The Company Shop

The Blaenafon Company shop in North Street near the Drum and Monkey Inn was owned and run by the Ironworks Company. This was the only shop in town and all the workers had to spend their hard earned cash there. Similar shops, known as 'Tommy Shops' existed at Garnddyrys and Pwll-du. On the 18th of February 1853 the Monmouthshire Merlin reported that they had ceased trading but eight years later the Garnddyrys and Pwll-du shops were being leased by John Harris and Co. However, they went bankrupt in 1863.

Approximate prices in the company shop in 1830:-

2lbs of mutton	1/-
2 lbs of beef	11d
1 lb of sugar	9d
1 lb of cheese	9d
2 lbs of bacon	1/6

Shopping was all done on credit which in due course was subtracted from the workers' weekly wages which were soon swallowed up and massive debts accumulated. Anti-truck laws later abolished the company shops which were undoubtedly the cause of much unrest and ill feeling.

In 1831 the wages of employees at Blaenafon were as follows:-

Colliers £1. 2. 6d. per week. Skilled Ironworkers £2. 15s - £3 per week. 7-9 year old boys earned about 4/6d per week. 9-16 year old boys earned about 10/- per week. Women were only rated at 7/6d per week.

In 1861 the 'Pontypool And Herald of the Hills Free Press' reported that "*a public meeting near the 'Big Stone' at Blaenafon considerd the high price of butchers' meat and at length passed unanimously a resolution - that no more fresh meat shall be produced by the working men of Blaenafon until it can be produced at sixpence per pound.*"

Mr. and Mrs. Bayliss who lived at Bunker's Row in 1900. Picture supplied by Francis Keen.

Blaenafon Pubs

At one time the people of this town used to boast that Blaenafon had so many pubs that you could drink in a different one every week of the year! This figure has now been reduced to less than one pub for every month of the year.

The furnace men consumed large quantities of liquid - particularly ale, for their work was extremely hot and regular thirst quenching was necessary. The most notorious of the local pubs was the Drum and Monkey Inn, North Street, which features in Alexander Cordell's novel. It should not be confused with the present day pub of that name on the old Black Rock road in the Clydach Gorge.

Also in North Street was the local 'clink' or 'lock up,' run by Mr. Hodder, Special Constable, whose name became corrupted very appropriately to Mr. Order. The 'lock up' was conveniently situated for drunks who needed calming down. Fighting in pubs was a regular occurrence, particularly on pay day when the men got well oiled!

The 'Lock Up'
Photograph supplied by
Francis Keen.

Decline of Blaenafon Ironworks

It used to be said that the world was girdled with Blaenafon iron and this was a reference to the great days of the railway age when Blaenafon was world famous for its superior quality iron rails which were in tremendous demand.

Three other British foundries even had an arrangement with the Blaenafon Company that allowed them to stamp the impressive words 'Blaenavon Iron Co.' on their rails which was a certain way of ensuring a good sales record. But by 1870 Blaenafon, had ceased to produce iron rails for the works was not able to compete with the high quality Bessemer rails which by then were being produced at Ebbw Vale.

In the late 1960s the National Coal Board sold the ironworks site to Blaenafon Urban District Council for land reclamation. Stack Square was declared unfit for habitation and the residents were rehoused. In 1972 the Department of the Environment took the site into their care and work started in 1974 on consolidating the site into a museum. This work is still being continued by Cadw.

CONTINUING THE WALK

5. Outside the ironworks, cross the road and turn right. (Notice the Ironworks Car Park opposite which provides an alternative starting point for this walk It is also very convenient if you just wish to visit Blaenafon Ironworks). Continue along the pavement to reach the Brynmawr Road. Turn left and shortly cross the road to follow a tarmac lane up to two houses. Just in front of the first house go up to a stile and on the other side ascend a short incline.

At the top of the incline on the right can be seen the remains of the braking system which controlled the rate of descent of the trams. Only a small part of this device remains to be seen, but it was obviously an ingenious system, well engineered and constructed of wrought and cast-iron. It was excavated in 1979 by John van Laun during a Department of Extra Mural Studies course sponsored by Cardiff University. Just to the north of the brake can be seen the remains of a small building which no doubt provided shelter for the brake man who operated a lever linked to the brake wheel.

6. The path soon joins another track which shortly levels out providing good views across to Coity Mountain and Big Pit. Across to the left can be seen the remnants of the village of Garn-yr-erw.

The area of land above Garn-yr erw is known as 'The Patches'. Here can be seen the surface workings where men once dug for ironstone which was found embedded in the shale. When these sources of ironstone became unprofitable to work, by the middle of the 19th century, the Blaenafon furnaces were fed with imported ores from Spain. It was found that the Spanish ores were more suitable than the Welsh material when used in the Bessemer furnaces which were introduced after 1860.

Stone stack at site of Hill Pits. Photographed in 1983 by Chris Barber.

7. **Walk on towards a stone stack** which is perfectly square and constructed of large blocks of stone. (SO 239102)

This is the site of Hill Pits which were sunk in the late 1830s to produce ironstone and coal for the Blaenafon Ironworks. It took its name from the hillside location (situated an an altitude of 1,420 ft above sea level) rather than the actual Hill family. The twin shafts were filled in about thirty years ago and the stone stack which is about 2 metres square and seven metre high was once linked to a boiler house.

The ironmaster were the pioneers of the Welsh coal trade because when it became difficult to obtain wood for fuel the iron trade declined until it was discovered that coalconverted into coke was an even better fuel than wood for smelting purposes. This resulted in a great revival in the coal trade.

Consequently the ironmasters did much to develop the mining of coal and sank many mines to supply themselves with coal to be used as coke in their great ironworks. The surplus coal was sold to other ironworks and it was not long before coal took over as an even more important and prosperous industry than ironmaking.

In its heyday Blaenafon was producing half a million tons of coal a year and its high quality steam coal was used in steam engines and steam ships all over the world.

8. Continue along the track to pass a pool with a small concrete dam. Just beyond here turn right to follow a well defined tramroad incline which heads straight up to the skyline. Be careful where you place your feet for the start may be wet and muddy in places.

This incline is half a mile long and it once consisted of four lines of rails. An engine with four wire ropes to haul the trams was mounted on the ridge. The system worked as follows:-

One truck was ready loaded at the bottom. Two trucks were on the summit (one full and one empty) and the truck at the Pwll-du side of the ridge was empty. In this position, and at the sound of a bell signal the engine would be set in motion and all four trucks would start moving at the same time. They were loaded at the Garn-yr-erw side and unloaded at Pwll-du.

9. Ascend the incline and on the skyline you will pass through a cutting to reach the crest of the ridge. Here you may enjoy extensive views across to the Brecon Beacons, the Black Mountains and the summit of the Blorenge.

The landscape here is scarred by opencast mining but the hollows in the ground have long since grassed over.

10. At a junction of tracks, go straight on and then down past a brick building. Unfortunately, sections of the old incline have been destoyed on this side of the hill, but tracks lead down towards a white building directly below, which is the Lamb and Fox Inn. There is a great atmosphere inside and this pub with its extensive views over the Usk Valley is well used by walkers and cavers.

11. From the inn follow a section of tramroad beside a stone wall and head towards the Blorenge aerials which can be seen on the skyline. Cross a rather boggy area and then head across to the site of the old Balance Pond. This once held the water that was used to operate a lifting system in a shaft cut into the face of the Pwll-du quarry, directly below this point. The old pond is now just a rectangular shaped stone lined hollow which has not held water for many years.

12. Walk along the edge of the pond to the far end and then follow a track down past a hollow and around a stone scattered depression, to decend diagonally to Hill's Tramroad (named after the ironmaster Thomas Hill). From here you can look across to Pwll-du Quarry where the masonry top of the Balance Shaft is clearly visible.

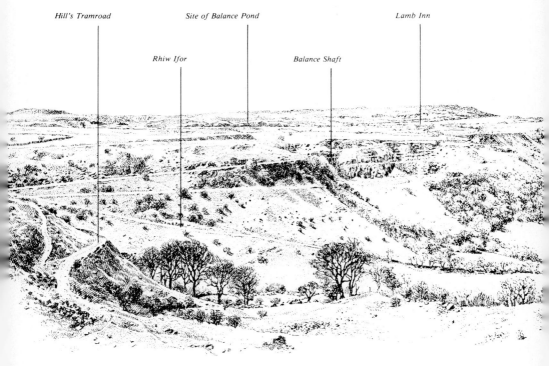

The head of Cwm Llanwenarth showing Hill's Tramroad and Pwll-du Quarry.

13. Turn right along Hill's Tramroad and walk towards Cwm Llanwenarth taking care not to walk too close to the edge of the track, where a steep drop was once guarded by an iron rail. Pausing at an opening in the trees, look across the valley to see the site of the old Garnddyrys Forge and the scattered ruins of the workers' cottages.

Try to imagine just what a busy and noisy place it must have been. In the distance can be seen the whaleback ridge of Skirrid Fawr and on the other side of the Usk Valley is the cone of Mynydd Pen y Fal (Sugar Loaf) looking for all the world like an extinct volcano.

14. **On reaching the head of the narrow cwm cross Rhiw Ifor** which was here long before the tramroads were even thought of, and scramble across the stream where the old bridge that once supported Hill's Tramroad has disintegrated. Then walk on past the ruins of a little stone building which once served as a blacksmith's shop (alternatively known as the Tumble Beer House).

If you look back from here you will see the convergence of tracks on the other side of Cwm Llanwenarth. Hills Tramroad curves around to the top of the Pwll-du Quarry and the lower track, which is now not very clearly defined, leads to the foot of the quarry. Cutting diagonally down the hillside is the prominent path of Rhiw Ifor which provided the original route into the valley.

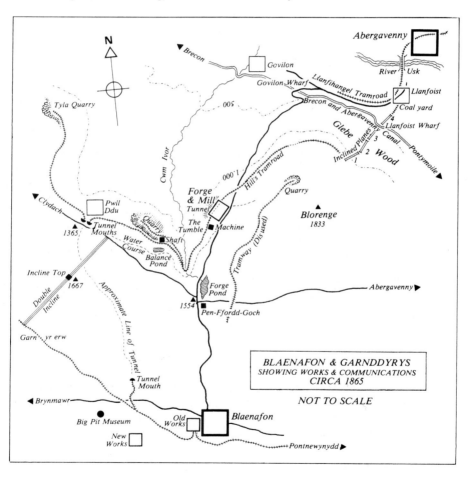

BLAENAFON & GARNDDYRYS
SHOWING WORKS & COMMUNICATIONS
CIRCA 1865

NOT TO SCALE

The main slag heap at Garnddyrys looking like a prehistoric monster but since this picture was taken by Chris Barber in 1985 the'head' has been removed by vandals.

15. The next section of tramroad is not very clear for it is hidden beneath a pile of boulders and earth which have slipped from the hillside above. Ahead of you is a strange looking heap of dark material which used to resemble a prehistoric monster. This is a heap of slag and it has been shaped by over a century of wind and rain. Sadly its 'head' has been vandalised in recent years with the result that it no longers resembles a chicken or frog or whatever creature different people saw in their imagination.

16. Leave the track which heads down past the pile of slag and walk across a level strip of land where the Garnddyrys Forge and Rolling Mill used to stand. Today, only the foundations of a few buildings can be seen and stonework on the right which was erected to support a pond directly above.

Situated at an altitude of 1,300 ft this must have been a wild and windy place to work especially in mid winter. During a week's operation some 300 tons of finished products were turned out here. Iron bars and rails were produced to be transported to many parts of Britain and countries throughout the world.

Above and to the right of the forge site were two ponds (now dry), each approximately one acre in area. They were constructed to supply water to the steam engines which were in use on the site. An outlet can be seen in the retaining wall of the upper pond. This was the supply point to the workings below. Unfortunately it was found that these two ponds were not large enough to supply sufficient water to efficiently operate both the forge and the mill so an additional pond was constructed at Pennford goch to provide additional water. A water channel may also be seen contouring around the hillside carrying water from the old coal levels at Pwll-du to top up the Garnddyrys ponds.

Water outlet in the western retaining wall of the Upper Pond. This was the supply point to the workings below.

An interesting feature below the Forge site is a short tunnel which was probably constructed to protect the tramroad from slag. It is about 6 ft 6 ins high, 8 ft 6 ins wide and the total length about 150 yards. There is a section of about 35 yards which can be entered through a hole in the side with care.

On 22 April 1853 a share holders meeting was held to decide the future of the Garnddyrys Forge and the following is an extract from the minutes book:-

"The works having now returned to a profitable condition the Directors have again seriously considered the best means of increasing the production of wrought iron, and at the same time of still further diminishing the expense of its manufacture. They are satisfied that this may be accomplished by the removal of the mill from Garnddyrys and its re-erection, with increased power and efficiency, on the Freehold Property of the Company at Blaenafon, and they desire to call the attention of the shareholders to their reasons for this conviction.

The site of the mill at Garnddyrys has been a constant cause of inconvenience and expense on account of its distance from the H.Q. at Blaenafon, and now that the Monmouthshire Canal Company have reduced their tonnages and improved the mode of conveyance along their road, these disadvantages are the most strikingly felt; the transit from Garnddyrys being by a circuitous and expensive route of twenty four miles, while the port of Newport will be reached by a locomotive railway from Blaenafon of only 16 miles.

The power of the present mill is scarcely equal to the production of 200 tons per week. It is proposed to make the new one, eventually, more than double that power, say equal to 500 tons per week, this increase, while tending to reduce the cost of the common charges upon each ton made, will enable the company to enter more largely into the manufacture of rails and to add that of 'Tyre Iron' and 'Boiler Plates' two articles for which the Blaenafon Iron is believed to be particularly well adapted.

Taking all these points into consideration the Directors have commenced this important alteration, as the means not only of increasing very materially the profit of the concern in favourable times, but what is of equally essential importance, of saving the company from losses in unfavourable years."

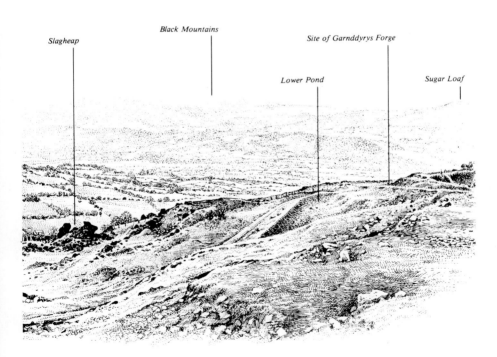

The site of Garnddyrys Iron Forge above Cwm Llanwenarth.

In 1860 the plant was dismantled and the rolling mill incorporated into a new works erected on the Coity side of Blaenafon at Forgeside.

"Garndyrus is gone, but the canal still stands as a tribute to her greatness; down which poured the thousands of tons that served the world."

A.C.

17. **Further on you will reach the site of the Garnddyrys Square** which consisted of 20 houses built on three sides of a triangle providing 5, 10 and 5 dwellings on the respective sides. By 1870 they had been partly demolished. A separate block known as Garnddyrys Row consisted of 15 houses in one block. By 1938 they were abandoned.

Another block was appropriately known as 'Ten Houses' and nearby were 'Pond Houses' which provided fourteen dwellings in two blocks of 6 and 8. They were probably built in about 1830. The families living on this site were largely Welsh but some came from Staffordshire and Ireland.

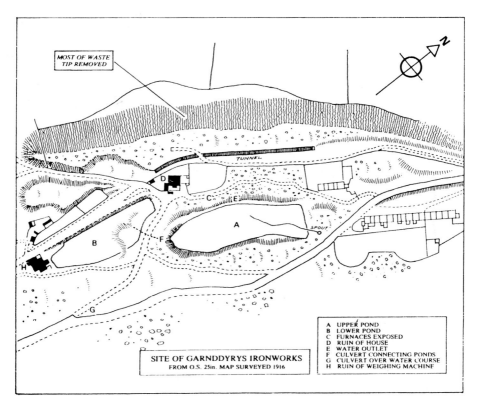

SITE OF GARNDDYRYS IRONWORKS
FROM O.S. 25in. MAP SURVEYED 1916

A UPPER POND
B LOWER POND
C FURNACES EXPOSED
D RUIN OF HOUSE
E WATER OUTLET
F CULVERT CONNECTING PONDS
G CULVERT OVER WATER COURSE
H RUIN OF WEIGHING MACHINE

18. **Go up to the Blaenafon Road and follow it down for about 100 yards and then cross it to continue along the tramroad, passing on your right the site of the old Queen Victoria Inn. In due course you will reach a shallow cutting which leads to a tunnel.** Adventurous walkers will choose to scramble down into it and tramp through the gloom and sheep droppings to the other side. If this does not appeal to you then follow the track over the top enjoying the panoramic view over the Usk Valley to the Black Mountains.

Hill's Tramroad on the north slope of the Blorenge near the top of the Llanfoist Incline.

On rounding a corner into the hollow on the north side of the Blorenge you will see a retaining wall on the right. It was at this point that the first section of incline descended on the left into Cwm Craf and near here a winch house was situated to control the descending trams. **This top section of incline is not a right of way, so continue along the track beside a fence and then head down towards a stile. From here head straight down towards the trees and follow a path leading steeply down through the wooded valley, to shortly join the next stage of the incline.**

Looking down 'The Big Drop' on the Llanfoist Incline.

19. Go over a stile and then on down to a platform where you will see a small brick hut. **From here the incline descends very steeply** and this section is known as 'The Big Drop.'

A brake wheel was set in a pit to control the descent of the trams down the incline. Passing around the brake wheel was a continuous chain which was fastened to the trams on each line of rails. Grooves cut by the passage of the chain may be observed on certain stones still in place on the incline.

Full trams descended under gravity pulling empty ones up on the other side. Accidents were frequent and were often cause by badly loaded and runaway trams. Between each stage of the incline was a platform where a brake wheel was sited and the trams were moved across to the next set of rails.

20 **At the bottom of the incline go over a stile and walk straight on to enter a tunnel** which passes under the Wharf Master's House and the canal. The noise of your boots echoes off the walls and mixes with the sound of a gurgling stream which flows into a channel on the right, once known as the 'Devil's Gully.'

If you wish to see Llanfoist Wharf go up some steps on the left to emerge on the canal towpath opposite the old Wharfmaster's House and Hill's Warehouse, which is known locally as the Boathouse. This was once a bustling scene of industrial activity where the trams from Garnddyrys were unloaded and the iron products transferred to the waiting narrow boats to be taken to Newport Docks or limestone and coal in the other direction to Brecon.

21. **Return down the steps and follow the lane down to Llanfoist village. If you wish to see the grave of the famous ironmaster Crawshay Bailey in Llanfoist churchyard go over a stile on the right** and in the far corner of the churchyard you will find a tall marble pillar with his name inscribed on it, and also that of his wife. Just behind the pillar is the grave of their faithful coachman.

Crawshay Bailey Senior was probably the most famous of all the ironmasters and with his brother Joseph developed one of the largest ironworks in the world at Nantyglo. On his retirement he lived in Llanfoist House and was 83 years old when he passed away.

Crawshay Bailey.

A hundred laughing people piling into the canal barges for their June outing to Newport Fair. *'The Garndyrus Benefit band was there; furnace men, colliers, quarrymen and limestone carriers in Sunday suits with their wives and children adorned in best dresses and lace, even if it meant going twice into debt at the shop.'*

WALK 2
Garnddyrys and Pwll-du
Allow (3 hours)

Park on the west side of the B4246, Blaenafon to Abergavenny road at Grid Reference SO 259122.

1. **Follow a wide track passing a large oval hollow on the right**. This is the site of a pond which once provided water used in the operation of the Garnddyrys Forge. The track zig zags down passing a lower pond site on the left, to join a fence. The views down into Cwm Llanwenarth are very impressive. Turn a corner and ahead will be seen a huge mound of slag which until it was unfortunately vandalised a few years ago, resembled a prehistoric monster. To the right of here is the site of the Garnddyrys Forge and Rolling Mill.

This industrial concern was only in operation for about half a century and only a comparatively small amount of information has come to light about its history. Many people might understandably wonder why a forge and rolling mill was established in this remote location and there are in fact three main reasons:-

a) When the Brecknock & Abergavenny Canal was linked with the Monmouthshire Canal at Pontymoile near Pontypool in 1812 it was a condition by Act of Parliament that goods transported via the B&A were charged the same rate as on the Monmouthshire Canal. Accordingly the Blaenafon Company, by transporting goods around the hillside and down to Llanfoist could achieve a substantial reduction in their shipment costs to Newport. By comparison the tolls on the Monmouthshire Canal via Pontnewynydd were excessive.

b) Limestone and coal were already being obtained from the Pwll-du side of the hill. This meant that trams could travel to a forge sited at Garnddyrys loaded with pig iron and then return via Pwll-du carrying coal and limestone.

c) In addition coal and limestone could also be transported in the other direction via a steep incline to Llanfoist where an added attraction was the proposed tramroad to Llanfihangel Crucorney. This would offer an opportunity for trade in the agricultural markets of Herefordshire. Coal and limestone could also be shipped up the canal to Brecon in one direction and the finished iron products from Garnddyrys could travel to Newport in the other direction. It was all a question of economics.

The land for the forge site was purchased in 1817 from William Price for £75 and the following year a long narrow strip of land for Hill's tramroad from Garnddyrys to Llanfoist was acquired from John Hanbury Williams.

Garnddyrys Forge in 1820.   Rough sketch drawn by Sir Richard Colt Hoare.

This little hillside forge turned out 300 tons of finished products in a week's operation. Iron bars and rails were produced which were transported to many parts of Britain and to various countries throughout the world. Horseshoes were also made here for the horses that worked by the Blaenafon Company.

"The Garndyrus furnaces are silent now; mere skeletons of greatness that nature by constant effort, is striving to obliterate. And it is difficult to believe, as one stands today on the crest of the Keeper's road that this was once a thriving community, a little town of people who lived their lives on the edge of a golden valley, who laughed and cried and brought forth children; who made iron of a quality incomparable; who sent their sons abroad to teach the art; whose sister town of Blaenafon sent her sons to Staffordshire to build new ovens, and as far abroad as Philadelphia..."A.C.

A re-construction of Garnddyrys Forge, immortalised by Alexander Cordell and now brought to life through the pen of Michael Blackmore. This is how it may have looked in about 1850. Billowing smoke rises from the tall chimneys of the puddling furnaces where the pig iron was converted into wrought iron and a rolling mill produced the final products such as bars, rails and plates. It is of interest that the iron for Crumlin viaduct was produced here in the 1850's.

2. **Walk around the pile of slag and follow the track downhill, ignoring any tracks on the right or left, to reach a metal gate, Go through and pass below the remains of a stone cottage**; its open doorway providing a basement shelter for damp sheep. The track leads down across a stream and through the fields. Look up to your right to see other ruined cottages that were once part of Garnddyrys village. The census of 1851 shows that about 300 people lived on this hillside.

3. **Pass through a gate by Blaen-y-cwm Farm and turn left down the drive. On reaching a road go straight across to follow a grass lane between stone walls to reach a footbridge spanning a rushing stream. Continue between hedges and past a barn to reach a gate. Cross another stream and follow a path ascending diagonally to the right between tumbled stone walls.** Through the trees on the right can be seen the distictive Skirrid Fawr (Ysgyryd Fawr), a sinister looking hill.

4. **In due course the track curves back to the left and steepens, now following an old incline leading up to the quarries on the hillside above. An unrelenting slope that may cause the unfit to puff and gasp a little, will thankfully, in due course, level out.** The reward is a fine view across Cwm Llanwenarth. Directly opposite is Garnddyrys and above will be seen your vehicle seemingly stuck with superglue to the hillside.

5. **Continue along the track below some limestone quarries to shortly reach a metal gate. Go through and the track ascends gently to bend right by another gate in a stone wall. Head up to meet an old tram road and follow it to the left (just below and parrallel to a gravel track) to reach a metal stile in a stone wall.** This stile is unusual for it has been constructed from old rails and girders and looks as if it should last for many years to come. **Continue beside a hedge and then through a gate.**

Soon you will see a low, bricked up archway on the right. This is the entrance to the Pwll-du tunnel which was constructed to connect the Blaenafon Iron Works with Garnddyrys Forge and was opened in about 1822. It was nearly one and a half miles long and the men who led the horse drawn trams through it, must have uttered many a curse, for this was the longest tramroad tunnel in Britain.

It was only single track and it must have become very congested, causing much wasted time and no doubt frequent accident must have occurred. So in due course a double incline was constructed over the hillside above. (See walk 4.)

Across to the left is the old village hall of Pwll-du which it is one of the few remaining buildings of this once thriving village. It is now used as an Adventure Centre. There were once two rows of terraced houses in this village known as 'Upper Rank' and 'Lower Rank' (or 'Short Row' and 'Long Row') comprising 14 and 28 houses respectively.

North portal of the Pwll-du tram road tunnel (SO 246116).

One of the Pwll-du pubs used to be the Prince of Wales where one bar was situated in Monmouthshire and the other in Breconshire, thus making it possible to have a drink on the same day in two counties in the same pub! At one time this pub was used as the company shop.

6. **On joining the Pwll-du road turn left and shortly take a gravel track on the left. It leads down to the old Lamb Inn** which has been reopened in recent years and re-named 'The Lamb and Fox'. Situated at an altitude of 420m (1377') it is one of the highest pubs in Wales. Walkers are made particualry welcome here and the landlord Brian Lewis has many fascinating tales to tell about life in the village when he was a boy.

7. **Leaving the Lamb and Fox Inn follow a section of tramroad beside a stone wall and head towards the Blorenge aerial which can be seen on the skyline. Cross a rather boggy area, where there are stones to step on if you can locate them, and head across to the site of the old Balance Pond.** This once held the water that used to operate a lifting system in a shaft cut into the face of Pwll-du Quarry, directly below this point. **Walk along the edge of the pond to the far end and then follow a track down past a hollow and around a stone scattered depression, to descend diagonally down to Hill's Tramroad.**

8. **This tramroad, named after the Ironmaster Thomas Hill is now followed around the head of Cwm Ifor with impressive views to be enjoyed. If you have young children with you take particular care, for there is a steep drop on the left of the wide track. Soon you cross a stream and the tramroad leads directly back to Garnddyrys. The slag 'monster' will be seen ahead and your car awaits you on the hillside above.**

WALK 3

Pwll-du Quarries
Allow (2.5 hours)

This route starts from the same location as Walk 2 on the side of the B4246 above Garnddyrys (SO 259122).

1. **Follow the track down overlooking the site of the upper pond. Leave the main track and follow a path down to the left of the pylons and descend beside the remains of an old stone wall to join Hill's tram road. Turning left, follow the tram road around to the head of the valley and cross the stream at the head of Cwm Ifor. On reaching a junction of tracks, follow a path descending to the right for about twenty yards and then take a narrow track on the left, maintaining height. This track is parallel to Hill's tram road and it crosses the hillside below a line of cliffs. Cross a stile and traverse around the steep slope to reach Pwll-du Quarry.**

A stream tumbles down the hillside to the left. Just to the right of this stream at ground level is a low entrance to a cave. It is a little daunting, but interesting to squirm inside to enter a small chamber and then duck under the low roof to stand up in a wide man made vertical shaft. (SO 251115), stretching skywards. It forms a fantastic echo chamber if you feel inclined to burst into song!

This shaft was cut through the limestone to enable a water balance lifting system to be installed which was used to raise loaded trams to a higher level. The water utilised to operate the system came from the Balance Pond higher up (visited on Walk 1).

A large wheel fitted with a powerful brake was fixed above the top of the shaft. It had a rope or a chain passing around it and to one end an empty cistern was attached which carried over it a tram filled with limestone. The other end of the chain was attached to a cistern which when filled with water was heavier than the loaded tram and the empty cistern combined.

The cistern was filled from a tank nearby and a brake regulated its descent. When it reached the bottom of the shaft a self acting valve would release the water which then escaped to the surface by an adit. The loaded tram on arriving at the top of the shaft was removed from the empty cistern which was then filled with water. Then the cistern at the bottom of the shaft was emptied and a loaded tram placed on it and so the process continued...

A group of quarrymen pictured near Pwll-du in 1880.   Picture supplied by Francis Keen.

2. **On leaving the cave go down a narrow cutting opposite to reach the edge of the escarpment and walk around to the left following a path overlooking Cwm Llanwenarth. Head for some hawthorn trees where a path winds around the edge of the slope to pass an iron boundary marker. Continue towards a television mast directly ahead (on Gilwern Hill). The path rises a little and then descends to join a path flanked by a post and rail fence. Turn right and follow the path with its metal hand rail down into the valley to reach a metal gate.**

3. **Continue across a field into a picturesque valley and join a tumbling stream. Walk on to a stone barn and go right over a stone bridge to follow a track down to a tarmac road. Turn right through a gate and follow the drive up to Blaen-y-cwm farm. Take the second gate on the right opposite a barn and follow the path up through the fields to reach a gate near a ruined cottage. Then bearing left carry on up a wide track to the site of Garnddyrys Forge and your starting point.**

WALK 4

Circuit of the Blorenge
Allow 4-5 hours.

Start from Keepers' Pond Car Park.

1. **Head up over fairly rough country following sheep tracks where possible, towards the tall aerials situated near the Foxhunter Car park. From this car park follow a tarmac path** to a memorial plaque which gives details of the many achievements of 'Foxhunter' - a famous show jumping horse whose skin was buried here by its owner Colonel Harry Llewellyn.

2. **Follow a well defined footpath in a north easterly direction to reach the summit of the Blorenge which is marked by a trig' point and a large cairn at an altitude of 559 metres (1,833'). Then continue in a north easterly direction to reach the edge of the escarpment overlooking Llanfoist and Abergavenny.**

3. **Follow a wide rutted track to the right which weaves in and out of a series of hollows and humps (old quary workings) and enjoy a new aspect towards the Coed y Prior woods. Further on the track divides. Keep on the wide path and follow it down to the Llanellen road.**

The Punchbowl.   Chris Barber 1985.

4. **Follow the road to the left, enjoying views into the peaceful valley below. After about 800 metres, go left by a cattle grid to follow a signposted bridle path. This wide track is followed for some distance, but just before some trees,**

where the path descends into a sunken lane, keep left and follow a track down through the field on the left to a gate. Then continue steeply down to meet a stone wall and follow this down, treading a thick carpet of leaves, beneath overhanging trees to suddenly emerge in a very beautiful location known as the 'Punchbowl'. In Welsh this natural depression is called Taren Cwm y Dison and it is of glacial origin. Before you is a pool reminiscent of a Lakeland tarn set beneath a natural ampitheatre clothed in trees. When the atmospheric conditions are right, a good echo can be obtained here by shouting with gusto at the hillside above. The Punchbowl is the site of a long forgotten quarry where sandstone was once extracted to be crushed into sand for use in the casting house at Blaenafon Ironworks.

Years ago this was a secret meeting place for the mountain fighters who used to come here to participate in prize-fighting contests. They fought with bare fists and generally wore the scars of previous fights on their broken-nosed faces. A look-out was always posted for the sport was illegal.

It was to the Punchbowl that Hywel Mortymer came one night in Cordell's novel, 'This Proud and Savage Land', when unemployed and penniless he endeavoured to win a few guineas in a prize fight.

"Money was chinking as new bets were laid: the body of my opponent was shining with sweat and his expression changed from surprise to pain as I circled him, shooting straight lefts through his guard, snapping his head back."

5. From the pool go up a short rise to a gate and then descend slightly through the next field, past a large heap of stones and on beside a fence. Go past a gate on the right (where a right of way leads down) and then ascend slightly, following the fence to reach another gate. Keep on beside the fence following a wide path to shortly reach another gate. A slight ascent and then the track starts to level out and the views from here are very rewarding. One looks over Abergavenny and across to the Sugar Loaf and Skirrid Fawr. It is possible to pick out some of the more easily identified buildings in the town such as the castle, Town Hall, Priory Church, Post Office, Nevill Hall Hospital etc..

"The path was lonely and pure with sunlight. Above us reared the mountain with its gorse fanning live in the wind and below us the valley of the Usk lay misted and golden at the foot of Pen-y-fal."

A.C.

6. Walk on around the eastern shoulder of the Blorenge and into the great northern bowl of the hill. Ignore the path ascending the steep slope above and head up to the right, aiming for the edge of a stone wall directly ahead. Then continue along Hill's Tramroad which was constructed in about 1820. It ran from the mouth of the Pwll-du tunnel to Garnddyrys Forge and then followed the 1200' contour line to the front of the Blorenge where it connected with the three inclined planes descending to

Llanfoist Wharf. It became redundant as a tramroad in about 1865 after the closure of the Garnddyrys Forge.

7. **Continue around the northern slopes of the Blorenge** enjoying a bird's eye view of Abergavenny and the Vale of Usk. On the left you will pass the remains of a small building and then a well constructed retaining wall. It was near this point that the top of the Llanfoist incline linked in with the tramroad.

You will observe holed stones which once supported the tramroad plateways. Sleepers were initially cast iron but it was found that these were brittle and liable to snap. Then wood was tried for a while without a lot of success and so in due course the iron plateways were mounted on stone blocks using iron saddles or chairs which were fastened to the stone blocks with iron spikes driven into oak plugs inserted in the block holes.

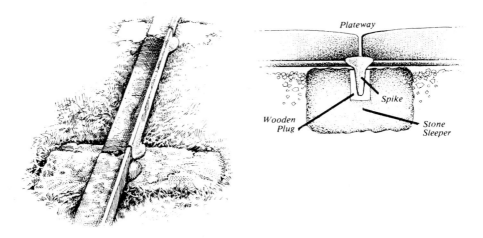

This illustration by Mike Blackmore shows how the tram plateways were spiked to the stone blocks.

Drivers of the horse drawn trams had to ensure that their loads did not stick out and if an accident occurred and the wagons were derailed the man had to get them back on the track as soon as possible. A jack or lever was generally carried for this purpose.

The rate of descent was controlled by means of a hardwood beam known as a 'sprag' which was positioned behind the rear wheels and a few inches above the track. By levering on the sprag and locking the rear wheels when required, speeds of up to fifteen miles an hour, with a load of five tons of limestone aboard could be achieved, although the official limit was just four miles an hour.

On the downhill journeys the horse was shackled behind the tram and allowed to gallop freely while the haulier controlled the downward descent of his load.

The view from here is most impressive. Beyond the Sugar Loaf can be seen the Black Mountain summits of Pen Cerrig Calch and Pen y Gader Fawr. As you progress along the tramroad the view extends even further up the Vale of Usk towards Mynydd Llangattock, Allt yr Esgair, Mynydd Llangorse and in clear weather the summit of Pen-y-Fan in the Brecon Beacons will show itself in the far distance.

8. Go through a shallow cutting which leads to a tunnel (which the adventurous may pass through with care, bending heads on entry). The track along the top soon dips down to the other side of the tunnel and the tramroad continues beside a leaning stone wall and contours around the hillside overlooking Cwm Llanwenarth. A diversion may be made from here by cutting down the hillside to take refreshment in the 'Cordell Country Inn', otherwise continue along the tramroad to meet the B4246.

Near the point where Hill's tramroad meets the B4246 used to stand the Queen Victoria Inn which was frequented by folk from Garnddyrys.

A man bought this inn just after the Second World War and went to the expense of installing electric light. He had a lively party there one night to celebrate the new improvements and whilst someone was thumping a rowdy song out on the piano the floor gave way and everyone including the piano fell into the cellar!

Pen-fford-goch Pond, locally known as the 'Keeper's Pond'.   Chris Barber 1985.

9. **Walk up the side of the road and then ascend a diagonal track on the left which leads up steeply at first and then flattens out to join an old quarry tram-road which is then followed to the right back to Pen-fford-goch pond.**

This pond was constructed in 1828 and was originally known as 'the Forge Pond'. It is about 2 acres in size and was built as a header pond to increase the water supply to Garnddyrys Forge. Later it became known as the 'Keeper's Pond', after the Keeper's Cottage which used to stand nearby. This little stone cottage was demolished in about 1970. The Keeper's job was to manage the Blorenge grouse moors which are the most southerly in Britain.

It was the Blaenafon Ironworks Company who built the spectacular road (B4246) descending the western side of the Blorenge in 1825. Before then the usual route from Abergavenny to Blaenafon was from Llanelen via the Lower and Upper Ninfa Farms. The new road was opened as a Turnpike route and gates were set up for the collection of tolls at Llanfoist, Garnddyrys and Cae White.

Pen-fford-goch means 'the head of the red road' and it would seem that Old Red Sandstone, which occurs in this vicinity was utilised in its construction. The red colour of the road was later even more apparent when red bunker ash from the Garnddyrys furnaces was used for repair work.

Hill's Tramroad at the head of Cwm Llanwenarth showing the old Blacksmilth's Shop which at one time was also known as the Tumble Beerhouse.

WALK 6

A bird's eye view of Blaenafon

Allow 3 hours. (Not including stops to visit places en route).

Start from the Blaenafon Ironworks car park (GR 248092)

1. **Go down some steps and turn right along the pavement which is followed down hill.** You will notice how the name of the Kennard family has been preserved in the town by such street names as Kennard Place and Kennard Crescent.

In 1836, Robert Kennard, a London banker, bought Blaenafon Ironworks Company and for the next seventy five years the Kennard family were virtually rulers of Blaenafon. The last of the Kennards was Company Chairman Arthur Kennard, who died in 1911. Their family motto 'Sed spes non fracta' - 'But hope is not broken' appears on the town crest.

2. **Continue down Church Road, passing Ty Mawr on the left**, which was built by Samuel Hopkins as his Blaenafon house. Locally Ty Mawr used to be referred to as 'The Big House' or sometimes 'Blaenafon House'. Samuel also had a second home in Nevill Street Abergavenny, where he stayed occasionally to enjoy the social life of the town. He bequeathed that property to his friend Dr. Steel, who was the Company Surgeon, and it is significant that the doctor's son was christened Samuel Hopkins Steel. In 1925 Ty Mawr became the local Medical Society's Hospital and today it is the Beeches Nursing Home.

On the right will shortly be seen the sad ruins of an old school which was built in 1816 by Sarah Hopkins in memory of her brother Samuel. It made history, for it was the first purpose built school in Wales to be established by an ironmaster for the benefit of the workers' children. John Coldwell was the first teacher employed there and when it opened he had 120 pupils. By 1850 this number had increased to 350, but Blaenafon's population had of course risen from 2,000 to 7,500.

Across the road will be seen the County Constabulary building and the impressive Blaenafon Workmen's Institute, which was built in 1894 and has recently been restored.

St Peter's Church is now seen on the right and this was built by the local ironmasters in 1804. The amount of iron used in its construction is a special feature of the building for the window frames, door sills, tomb covers and even the font are all made of this durable material. The church itelf is built in a plain Gothic Revival style.

Before this church was constructed, Samuel Hopkins used to hold church services in his house and as both he and his sister were Welsh speaking, and most of the Blaenafon people did not understand English, the services were conducted entirely in Welsh.

The first vicar of St Peter's was the Rev. James Jenkins and he remained there from 1805 when the church was first opened, to his retirement thirty seven years later. He was succeeded by the Rev. John Jones who resided in the first vicarage which stood near Glantorfaen Terrace and he lived there for forty five years until he died at the age of seventy five. He could preach in English and Welsh and he conducted services in St Peter's at 11.00 a.m. and 6.00 p.m. on Sunday in English and in-between, at 3.00 p.m. he was at Capel Newydd preaching in Welsh. As chapel services were at 9.00 a.m., many chapel folk would then flock to church to hear John Jones preach after their own services were over.

An interesting entry in the parish register records on 7 June 1812, the death of Richard Morris, aged 55 years, a native of North Wales who died at Nantyglo after being bled to death by a quack doctor.

On the wall inside the church is a monumental inscription commemorating one of the town's best loved doctors. It reads:-

Sacred to the memory of Dr. Samuel Elmes Steel,
Surgeon of Blaenafon Ironworks, who was accidently
killed by a fall from his horse, whilst discharging
his professional duties on 29th day of July 1867
in the 34th year of his age.

This memorial tablet has been erected by the inhabitants
of the above place to testify their regard and regret
for a man held in much esteem and repute. His loss will
long be felt and deplored by all who love him.

The Steel family were the first medical men to come to Blaenafon. In the beginning, Doctors' Thomas, William and Christopher Steel visited the town alternately three times a week from Abergavenny and in cases of emergency they would come more often. Their surgery was located just below the Company stables.

But in due course there was a demand for a resident doctor and Dr. Richard Steel, who had been a doctor in the navy, became the first resident medical man in Blaenafon. By all accounts he was an able and clever doctor.

Both Thomas Hill and Thomas Hopkins are buried in the church and they are commemorated on a wall tablet as follows:-

'Sacred to the memory of Samuel Hopkins, Esquire of Blaenafon,
Where in conjunction with his much respected relative and partner
Thomas Hill, Esquire of Dennis, Staffordshire, he founded the
Ironworks and builded and endowed this church. The benevolence
and utility of his character were great and uniform, because they were founded on
the principles of Christianity. He died June Vth MDCCCXV.

This tablet was placed here by his sole and truly attached sister Sarah Hopkins.'

Sarah Hopkins School   Chris Barber 1989

Blaenafon Wokrmen's Institute was built in 1894 and has recently been restored.   Chris Barber 1996.

In a vault adjoining the church are the remains of Thomas Hill Esquire of Blaenafon:

'The kind and affectionate father of five children, who survive to lament their severe loss and by whom this tablet is erected to his reverend memory. He died Nov 29th, 1827, aged 59.'

St. Peter's Church, Blaenafon.   Chris Barber 1984.

St Peter's Church was where Iestyn amd Mari were married in 'Rape of the Fair Country'....

"The bells were ringing joyfully, the sun blazed down. It was a happy, golden wedding day. The church was crowded, even the balcony was filled, and the tall hats of the women came round as we walked in and up the long red carpet to the altar..."

3. **After visiting the church, continue past the post office and go right beside the Queen Victoria Inn. Walk around the corner and turn right to follow the road at the bottom of St Peter's Church graveyard. Carry on past a small housing estate and then via a pavement and a short section of road to shortly turn left and cross the 'iron bridge'.**

Below, the Afon Lwyd tumbles on its way down the Eastern Valley to eventually join the Usk at Caerleon. Afon Lwyd translates as the Grey River, but it was once so polluted that it should have been named the black river. Originally it was known as the Torfaen from which the local authority takes its name. The source of the river can be found near Garn-yr-erw.

4. **Follow a path from the bridge and go left up Forgeside Road. On a bend cross the road and ascend some steps to follow a path up to a metal kissing gate. Turn right and walk along the road enjoying a good view over Blaenafon and the surrounding area.**

5. **Cross a bridge spanning the old railway line and follow a pavement up to a T junction.** (Forgeside Inn to the right was previously called the 'Footballer's Arms' in tribute to Ken Jones a well known rugby player, who was born in Blaenafon). **Go straight across the road and over a stile on the other side to ascend a gravel track. This bridle path takes you up past a drift mine and below to the right can be seen the hamlet of Forgeside**

These terraces of cottages were unimaginatively named ABCD and E, but A and B rows have been replaced with new houses and re-named.

Forgeside Iron and Steel Works in about 1905.   Picture supplied by Francis Keen.

Blaenafon Ironworks Company employees at Forgeside 1895   Francis Keen Collection

The new works at Forgeside was commenced in 1858 and opened in 1860. It had many advantages over the old Blaenafon Ironworks. For a start access was easier and there was more space for future development on a fairly level site.

The Garnddyrys Forge had proved very inconvenient being so far from the Blaenafon Company Headquarters and also the distance from Garnddyrys to Newport via the difficult and dangerous inclines and the slow canal was 26 miles. By comparison the distance from Blaenafon to Newport by the new railway down the Eastern Valley was only 16 miles.

Six blast furnaces were constructed on the Forgeside site and a tyre mill was also built to produce wheels for railway rolling stock. The new works was constructed on freehold land and consequently there was no longer any requirement for the Company to pay ground rent to Lord Abergavenny.

By 1880 the Blaenafon Ironworks had been developed to such a standard that it was regarded as the most modern ironworks in the world. In that year Blaenafon was described as 'a place with an extensive ironworks, abundant collieries, seven blast furnaces and three rolling mills for heavy and light rails, four brick factories, and the adoption of the electric light.

The last furnace at Forgeside, Blaenafon was extinguished in 1938. The local reserves of iron had long been depleted and the cost of transporting imported iron ore from the coast to the works high up the Eastern Valley had become too expensive. The future now lay in the erection of new large steel works in the coastal regions of South Wales.

6. On reaching a bend keep straight on through a gate to follow a grass track which soon becomes rutted and often wet. It leads on beside a fence. Continue past a ruined building and head up to join a wide track which snakes around the hillside above. Turn right and follow this track. The views from here are excellent taking in the whole of Blaenafon while across to the left the Black Mountains can be seen. Soon you are looking down on Big Pit.

Big Pit Mining Museum.   Chris Barber 1996.

Sunk in about 1840, this was one of the oldest pits in the South Wales coalfield. It derived its name from its unusually wide shaft which is about 18 ft across. In its heyday this mine employed 2,000 men and produced half a million tons of coal a year. It was a non-gassy mine which produced steam coal of top quality which was used in the local ironworks.

At one time Blaenafon had thirty five collieries and Big Pit was the last one to survive. In 1970 there were 494 men employed here - working in a single seam - the 2' 6" Garw seam. By 1979 the work force had been reduced to 250, and in 1980 the reserves were finally exhausted so the pit closed. However, this was not the end of the story, for today it is a unique mining museum which is visited by 100,000 people every year. The underground tour involves descending in the pit cage down a 300 ft shaft. Some of the men who previously worked here as miners are now employed as guides and they are pleased to relate to the visitors their memories of working underground.

7. Three lakes come into view. The nearest one is a long and narrow industrial water supply, while the two other rounded ponds have been created as the result of a landscaping scheme.

Across the valley can be seen the remnants of Garn yr erw village, where Lower Garn and Upper Garn terraces still stand. Below these houses there was once a farm called Ty Rebeka which took its name from the time when it was damaged by the Rebecca rioters in 1840.

The track joins a tarmac road which has been built to provide access to a drift mine higher up (notice the entrance to a disused mine dated 1966 on the left). **Follow the tarmac road** with the summit of the Sugar Loaf coming into view, while directly below is a steam railway run by the Pontypool and Blaenafon Railway Society. They are a band of enthusiasts who spend their spare time re-establishing the old railway, restoring old locomotives, rolling stock and providing steam train rides for visitors.

This line was originally opened in 1869, and was part of the London and North Western Railway between Brynmawr and Pontypool which joined the Great Western Railway at Abersychan. It was closed to passengers in 1941 but the line from Blaenafon to Pontypool carried coal from Big Pit and other local mines until 1980.

With the usual short sightedness, the 'powers that be' lifted the track from Pontypool to just south of Blaenafon High Level Station soon after its closure. But the Railway Society operate a train ride as far as the Whistle Inn where a new platform has been constructed. They hope in due course to relay the track to Waunafon which, at 1400 ft above sea level, was once the highest main line station in England and Wales. At one time it was possible to travel from approximately sea level at Newport to 1,400 ft at Waunafon and then drop down through Brynmawr and the Clydach Gorge to Abergavenny which is just 10 ft above sea level.

8. Follow the tarmac road around uphill for a short way. It shortly cuts through a diagonal track which is now followed down to the right and on to the Whistle Inn. Yes, no doubt you have already thought of it - this is an excellent place to 'wet your whistle', just as Iestyn Mortymer did on his way to his wedding at St. Peter's Church, Blaenafon.

"Mari Dirion! How lovely was her name. I said it aloud to the rhythm of Elot's hoof beats on the mountain turf. Spurring her, we made a gallop to swing across the mountain to the Whistle Inn. A pint to settle the dust, a pail of spring water for Elot, and a sleep beneath a tree..."

9. **Suitably refreshed, follow the road from the Whistle Inn to join the B4248. Turn right and walk along the verge to shortly cross a cattle grid. After about 100 yards go up a gravel track on the left, which leads through a gate and heads up towards the spoil heaped hillside. At a junction of tracks, keep on the middle stony path and go up between the spoil heaps. Turn right at the next junction and ascend to join a broad level track. This is now followed to the right.**

Shortly on the left will be seen the long incline passing over the hill to Pwll-du and built by Thomas Dyne Steel in 1850, to supersede the old tram road tunnel. A stone stack on the right marks the site of Hill Pits.

To the left, a ruined building will be seen on the hillside. This is known as Ty Abraham Harry and was once a farmhouse. It is named after the original occupier who is said to have extracted coal from near here which was put in sacks and transported by mule.

In due course on the left at the top of a short incline, will be seen the remains of a braking system which once controlled the rate of desent of the trams.

10. **Go down to the B4248 and turn left. Shortly go right and follow the road back to your starting point.**

Big Pit, Blaenafon.

WALK 6

Capel Newydd and the Goose and Cuckoo
Allow 2 hours (not including the pub stop!)

1. Take the old Llanover road from Blaenafon and park just above the site of Capel Newydd (GR. 270077). There is a wooden seat just below the road which from this point bends up towards the crest of the ridge.

The site of Capel Newydd is marked by an iron cross set in a concrete plinth. It was Blaenafon's first church and is marked on a map published in 1600. At one time there was a stone in the churchyard bearing the date 1577, so a church was in existence for over three hundred years at the very least. The last sermon was preached here one Sunday in 1861. It was in Welsh, for no other language had been used for services in this chapel. In 1863 the building was dismantled and the stone used for building St Paul's Church in Blaenafon.

2. Go up the road a short way and then turn right along a bridle path, just above the forestry plantation. The rutted track leads along a heather-clad hillside to pass beneath some electricity pylon wires.

In the early years of the 19th century, this track was used by packhorses or mules carrying iron ore to the Hanbury furnaces at Pontypool. These beasts of burden were operated in teams of twelve and each animal carried about three hundred weight.

The ore was excavated in patches on Elgam Hill on land leased by the Hanbury family from the Nevills of Abergavenny. 'Patches' were deep holes dug in the ground to reach the coal and iron seams which lay just beneath the surface.

To the right can be seen Mynydd Farteg Fawr and the community of Varteg. In the distance is Abersychan and the Bristol Channel may be seen far ahead, gleaming in the sunlight.

3. Turn left at well defined crossing of tracks (about 100 metres before a radio mast), and head up to a shallow col on the ridge, following a well trodden path which was once used by folk crossing the ridge between Cwmavon and Llanover.

On reaching the crest of the ridge, you may see ahead, the distinctive profile of Skirrid Fawr, the hump of Graig Syffrydin and the Blorenge summit on the left.

4. Keep straight on and descend between intricately constructed stone walls, obviously built by highly skilled craftsmen. Go through a gate and carry on down beside a wall; then down a stony path to reach another gate. Keep straight on at the next track junction and descend a tree-lined hollow lane, crunching through the brown leaves of countless autumns. Another gate is reached and then a cart track is followed to reach a tarmac road which leads down to the Goose and Cuckoo Inn.

The Goose and Cuckoo Inn.   Chris Barber 1987.

This is Llanover's only surviving pub, for in the 19th century, Lady Llanover, who was a fervent teetotaler closed the other six and turned them into coffee houses. Fortunately this one was outside her estate and the owners refused to sell it to her.

5. **Leaving the Goose and Cuckoo, return up the road for a few hundred yards and take the farm drive on the right, leading down to Hendre Glyn Farm, which nestles in the valley below. Follow the drive over a chattering brook and then go through a gate on the left to ascend a broad track in the field above. Pass through a gate and observe the interesting conglomerate rocks scattered about the field. When the track flattens out,** look to the right to see, near a farmhouse, a conical shaped construction. This is a beehive pigsty, a type once common in Wales.

6. **Go through a gate and turn left along the road, which is followed over the ridge and through the 'mountain gate' which has been replaced by a cattle grid.** Ahead, if the visibilty is good, will be seen the summits of the Brecon Beacons. Follow the road back to your starting point.

WALK 7

Ty Mawr and Crawshay Bailey's Towers
Allow 1.5 hours

To reach the starting point of this walk from Brynmawr; drive south along the old road to Abertillery to reach Nantyglo. Turn right by the Wesleyan Chapel (by sign post to 'Round Towers') to reach Roundhouse Close. Take the second turning to the left and then shortly bear right along a gravel track. Soon you will see a round stone tower directly ahead. There is a small space for parking on the side of the track just before the tower.

1. Walk along the track to the left of the tower and shortly branch left to pass some houses. Follow the track around the left and go down to a gate in the fence on the roght which gives access to the site of Ty Mawr, otherwise known as Nantyglo House.

The northern Round Tower
built by the Bailey brothers
at Nantyglo in about 1816.

Nantyglo House in about 1900.   Picture supplied by Trevor Rowson.

This was an impressive mansion built by the Bailey brothers. They chose an elevated but sheltered site near the small house built by Mr. Harford who was the first ironmaster of the Nantyglo works and his home was subsequently turned into servants' quarters.

Ty Mawr had a fine colonnaded front supported by six iron pilars cast in the Bailey's own works, and inside was a magnificent marble staircase. The grounds were beautifully landscaped and the driveway passed through an impressive avenue of trees.

The Bailey brothers must have felt uneasy in their great mansion, particularly after the Merthyr uprising in 1813 and in order to protect themselves and their families from their own workers in times of trouble, they constructed in about 1816, two fortified towers. To provide immediate access it is claimed that they even linked the mansion with one of the towers by constructing an underground passage. However this tunnel has yet to be discovered.

In 1830 Joseph Bailey retired from the management of the works and moved to Glan Usk Estate near Crickhowell. Crawshay Bailey continued to live at Ty Mawr until 1860 when he retired to Llanfoist House.

Ty Mawr was then occupied by the managers of the Nantyglo and Blaina Iron and Coal Company until 1885. After that date it ceased to be lived in, and gradually became a ruin. During the Second World War it was demolished and the stone used for building purposes and road construction. The site of Ty Mawr has been excavated by Nantyglo Comprehensive School and also men employed on a Manpower Services Commision Scheme.

The southern Round Tower before the stonework was made safe in recent years.   Chris Barber 1987.

2. Retrace your steps a short way and follow a rising path beside a fence / stone wall, leading up through the trees. On reaching a wide track turn left and follow it to reach a gate near some picnic tables. Once through the gate go over a stile on your right and then on between fences; soon climbing steeply to reach another stile. The large house in the trees over to the left is Coalbrookvale, once the home of George Brewer, another ironmaster.

Nantyglo Ironworks in 1820.

3. From the stile head straight up to to join a wide track and turn right.

This is a good vantage point. Below can be seen the two round towers and the large stable block where the Baileys kept their horses and carriages. To the north can be seen the sprawling town of Brynmawr, which is the highest town in Wales, where winter comes early and is very prolonged. Beyond Brynmawr is the mass of Mynydd Llangynidr which is honeycombed with caves.

The valley below was once dominated by the massive Nantyglo Ironworks belching smoke and flames to the sky. It was opened in 1795 and subsequently purchased by Joseph Bailey in 1811. His brother Crawshay joined him as a partner in 1813. Under their joint ownership the works quickly developed into one of the largest and most efficient in the world and the two brothers soon amassed a fortune.

When Crawshay Bailey died in 1872 the Nantyglo works was sold to the Nantyglo and Blaina Ironworks Company for £300,000, but it eventually closed in 1878 and was entirely dismantled. All the machinery and even scraps of iron was sold off to meet the demands of the creditors. Only the empty buildings were left, but they were demolished many years ago and there is nothing to be seen of this once great ironworks today.

"This was the Bailey empire where the iron bubbles into a thousand moulds. Sweat pours here, beer is taken by the gallon, men die in mutilation, children are old at ten. Eyes are put out, sleeves are tied with string. The turrets of the ironmaster's house were stark black against the glow, the windows glinting, his defence towers threatening any challenge. From Cwm Crachen to Coalbrookvale was a river of fire."

A.C.

4. **Decend slightly to a stile in the fence on the left and then follow a path on the edge of the Nantyglo Golf Course.** This is the highest golf course in England and Wales where the 14th hole is at an altitude of about 1500' and is known as the 'Crows Nest'!

5. **Follow a path down to join a gravel track** which descends past numerous shacks where chickens wander freely. This is not a very tidy landscape but it provides a fascinating insight into the life of the Nantyglo hill folk. **On reaching a tarmac road, turn right to walk back to your starting point.**

"There is no green on the mountain after dark. Sulphur is in the wind then, and the sky is red with furnace glare all over the ridges from Nantyglo to Risca and when the nightshift comes on the world catches alight."

A.C.

DATES OF LOCAL INDUSTRIAL EVENTS

1782	The Blaenafon Coal and Iron Company is formed by Thomas Hill and Samuel Hopkins.
1789	The first furnace in Blaenafon comes into operation.
	Nantyglo Ironworks opens.
1790-92	Blaenafon Ironworks produces an average of 3,600 tons of iron per year.
1795	Tram road constructed from Blaenafon Ironworks to Pontnewynydd.
1796	Output at Blaenafon Ironwork is increased to 4,138 tons per year.
1798	Monmouthshire Canal completed (Newport to Pontypool)
1800	Archdeacon Coxe visits Blaenafon.
	Population in Blaenafon is 1,000.
1802	Monmouhshire Canal is extended to Pontnewynydd.
1805	St. Peter's Church in Blaenafon is built by Thomas Hill and Samuel Hopkins.
1811	Nantyglo Ironworks is sub-let to Joseph Bailey, Crawshay Bailey and Matthew Wayne.
1812	Brecon and Abergavenny Canal is joined with Monmouthshire Canal.
	14,579 tons of iron are sent by canal to Newport during this year.
1815	Battle of Waterloo. This is followed by an industrial slump in Britain.
	Death of Samuel Hopkins.
1816	Welsh Ironmasters make threats to reduce wages. The workers down tools and hold meetings. A school is built in Blaenafon by Sarah Hopkins in memory of her brother Samuel.
1824	Death of Thomas Hill the first.
1825	Turnpike road from Blaenafon to Abergavenny is constructed (now the B4246).
	Nantyglo becomes the leading iron producing works in Monmouthshire.
1827	'Garn Derris Iron Compan'y is formed.
	Death of Thomas Hill the second.
1828	Forge Pond constructed (now known as Keeper's Pond).
1829	Anti-Chartist meeting held at Coalbrookvale with Crawshay Bailey in the chair.
1830	Skilled ironworkers at Blaenafon are now earning £2.15s per week.
	9,937 tons of iron from Blaenafon is transported by canal. The figure for the same year from Garnddyrys is 3,654 tons. (Between 1817-1840 the Garnddyrys figure is 94,808 tons).
1836	R.W. Kennard takes over the Blaenafon Ironworks and forms the Blaenafon Coal and Iron Company Ltd.
1837	The Peoples' Charter is drawn up by the Chartists.
1838	A 'lock up' is built in North Street, Blaenafon.
	14 men and 2 women drown in Cinder Pit, Blaenafon.
1839	3/4 November Chartists' uprising and march on Newport.
	Mass trial of the Chartists held at Newport.
1842	Mines Act passed by Parliament.
1847	Forgside Works is established for smelting operations.
1850	Blaenafon-Pwll-du incline is reconstructed by Thomas Dyne Steel to use standard gauge waggons.
	Population of Blaenafon is now 4,000.
1852	The Great Western Railway Line from Newport to Pontypool is completed.

1853	Decision made to move the forge at Garnddyrys to Forgeside, Blaenafon.
1854	Blaenafon to Pontypool Railway is opened.
	John Frost the Chartis leader receives an unconditional pardon.
1856	Henry Bessemer invents a new process for making steel.
1857	Crumlin Viaduct is opened. Blaenafon iron was used for this enormous project.
1860	Garnddyrys Forge is dismantled.
	Population of Blaenafon is 7,500.
	Big Pit is opened.
1862	Blaenafon Town Hall is opened in Lion Street.
	New forge in operation at Forgeside.
1867	Dr. Samuel Steel, surgeon of Blaenafon Ironworks dies after falling off his horse.
1868	Riots break out in Blaenafon during the General Election.
	The LNWR line is opened between Blaenafon and Brynmawr.
	Death of Thomas Hill the third.
1870	Elementary Education is made compulsory for children.
1872	Crawshay Bailey Jnr. restores Llanfoist Church in memory of his father.
1873	The Blaenafon Company are operating 16 collieries in addition to the ironworks.
1877	Death of John Frost.
	Sydney Gilchrist Thomas and Percy Gilchrist carry out experiments at the Blaenafon works to reduce the phosperous content of steel.
1879	Blaenafon Ironworks Company is reformed and the name is shortened to Blaenafon Company Ltd., with a new board of directors.
1880	Blaenafon Ironworks is rated as the most modern in the world.
	Andrew Carnegie an American ironmaster pays 25,000 dollars for the Gilchrist Thomas formula.
	Great Western Railway take over the stock of the Monmouthshire Railway and Canal Company.

"Iron accomodates itself to all our wants, our desires, and even our caprices; it is equally serviceable to the arts, the sciences, to agriculture, and war; the same ore furnishes the sword, the ploughshare, the spring of a watch or of a carriage, the chisel, the chain, the anchor, the compass, the cannon, and the bomb. It is a medicine of much virtue, and the only metal friendly to the human frame.'

Dr. Ure 1841.

The Bridge Inn, Llanfoist

welcomes you to a beautiful waterside setting.
The Bridge Inn rests on the banks of the River Usk
with panoramic views across Castle Meadows.
Just five minutes from the village of Llanfoist,
with its canal side walks and meandering cycle tracks.

Join us on a Summer evening for a bar-b-que
or sample one of our home cooked meals from our
extensive menu, all freshly prepared by Andrew and Sian.
Parties are catered for (please Book in advance)
and children are most welcome.

Tel: Andrew & Sian on - 01873 853045

The Goose & Cuckoo Inn

Tel: 01873 880277

A real ale pub situated in a quiet hillside location
900 ft above sea level.
Extensive Views

Muddy boots welcome.
Great atmosphere and unusual food.

John and Anne look forward to seeing you soon!

The Whistle Inn

Circa 1792

Cliff & Rose Herbert
Tel: 01495 790403

REAL ALE. BAR MEALS. TRADITIONAL SUNDAY LUNCH

CHILDREN WELCOME

Large Collection of antique miners' lamps on view

Walkers always made particularly welcome

BARA BRITH TEAROOMS

Lakeside, Garn-y-Erw, Blaenafon

Tel: 01495 792299

Walkers made welcome

Delicious home baked cakes and scones
Tea Gardens and Car Park

Resident Psychic available for readings

PUBLICATIONS BY BLORENGE BOOKS

Blorenge Books publish books about Wales and in particular the area covered by the ancient kingdom of Gwent. Copies of the following titles may be obtained by writing to Blorenge Books and enclosing cheques (made out to Blorenge Books) for the relevant amounts:-

Hando's Gwent Volume II by Chris Barber......................................£7.50
The Ancient Stones of Wales by Chris Barber and John Williams....£7.95
Journey to Avalon by Chris Barber & David Pykitt.........................£9.90
The Seven Hills of Abergavenny by Chris Barber........................... £5.25
Stone and Steam in the Black Mountains by David Tipper...............£5.75
Arthurian Caerleon by Chris Barber...£3.99

Blorenge Books, Blorenge Cottage, Church Lane, Llanfoist
Abergavenny NP7 9NG
Tel: 01873 856114

TO BE PUBLISHED LATER IN 1996

'On the Trail of the Chartists'

This book will be a companion volume to 'Walks in Cordell Country'. It will deal specifically with the Chartists uprising and will again relate to Alexander Cordell's novel 'Rape of the Fair Country'. In this book Chris Barber sets out to unravel the events leading up to the Chartists' march on Newport to storm the Westgate Inn in November 1839. Some walks are included which the reader may follow and details of interesting locations involved in this important historic event.

'Portraits of the Past'

Compiled by Chris Barber and illustrated by the well known artist Michael Blackmore, this book tells the story of the industrial history of Monmouthshire which at one time was one of the greatest iron producing areas in Britain.

Packed with beautiful and detailed illustrations, 'Portraits of the Past' provides a fascinating record of ironworks, tramroads, canals, collieries and railways established in this county during the days when, raw materials, engineering expertise and manpower were combined to produce a social and economic revolution.

It is to be published as a 'coffee table' book and will be a much prized possession at a cost of £19.95. Reserve your copy of this very special book by sending a deposit of £5 to Blorenge Books (address as above).

What they said about Cordell Country:-

"Cordell Country in discovering the heritage of the ironmaking communities immortalised in 'Rape of the Fair Country' enlightens and educates at the same time, as it points you on your way. "

Terry Campbell - Western Mail 1985

"Chris Barber has done the cause of Welsh tourism a great service by writing 'Cordell Country'. This is a lovely area to visit, and Chris Barber's book provides the ideal springboard for a walking holiday. But read 'Rape of the Fair Country before you go."

Peter Evans - Great Outdoors Magazine 1985

"Inspired by Cordell's seductive prose and Chris Barber's own obvious spiritual affinity with the countryside he describes, the reader at home or out, tracing the recommended paths is utterly captivated..The illustrations by Michael Blackmore are great"

Mike Rice - South Wales Argus 1985